I Can Be Fair!

by David Parker
Illustrated by Meredith Johnson

SCHOLASTIC INC.
New York Toronto London Auckland Sydney
Mexico City New Delhi Hong Kong Buenos Aires

To every person that reads this book, thank you.
— D.P.

For Olivia and her little sister, Brooke.
— M.J.

ISBN 0-439-79209-6

Text copyright © 2005 by David Parker
Illustrations copyright © 2005 by Meredith Johnson
All rights reserved. Published by Scholastic Inc.
SCHOLASTIC, THE BEST ME I CAN BE™ Readers, and associated logos are trademarks and/or
registered trademarks of Scholastic Inc.

12 11 10   7 8 9 10/0

Printed in the U.S.A.
First printing, October 2005

Being fair is sometimes hard to do.

I can be fair and share with my friends.

I can be fair and let someone else choose first.

I can be fair and clean up my mess.

Being fair is sometimes hard to do.

I can be fair and take turns when I play.

I can be fair and tell the truth.

I can be fair and sometimes go last.

Being fair is sometimes hard to do.

I can be fair and make two equal teams.

I can be fair and not always get my way.

I can be fair and not leave anyone out.

Being fair is sometimes hard to do.
But being fair helps people get along.

What will you do to be fair today?